Warriors: Our Battle Cry

Warriors: Our Battle Cry

Nikki Robbs

God's Glory

ISBN: 9781790700929

Table of Contents

Welcome Letter (Introduction)

———— ❦ ————

Hey, you! Welcome to the journey that will leave you feeling equipped and ready to take on any battles that come your way. I am so excited to get started! If I could hug you through this page, I would hug you a million times because I am ecstatic for your eyes and heart to be open for the Lord to move on your behalf. All you need is your Bible, a notebook for notes, and an open heart to read through this study and get the most out of it. There will also be room left for you to write down revelations and prayers at the end of your devotion. We will read Bible passages and focus on certain verses, so take down as many notes as you need. Write down anything that speaks to your heart. Each day will be set up like we are physically training. There will be a passage from the Bible to read as your warm-up, a scripture of focus to memorize, words of encouragement to exercise your spiritual muscles, and a challenge for you to take on during your day. Get all those things handy, and let's get started!

Armor Up

⎯⎯⎯ ∞∞∞ ⎯⎯⎯

THIS WEEK WE WILL DISCUSS Ephesians, chapter 6, and break down each piece of the Lord's armor we need in order to be the spiritual warriors we are called to be. Notice I said the Lord's armor: "Therefore, put on every piece of God's armor so you will be able to resist the enemy in the time of evil" (Eph. 6:13). Therefore, as you go from day to day with the study this week, remember that you are being gifted with God's armor—not just any hand-me-down, cheap armor but the Lord's. We cannot move forward into battle claiming victory without the right equipment. After this first week, you will then be prepared to move through the rest of this study. I have no doubt Satan will try to distract you and prevent you from finishing the weeks or even days. I am in prayer for you, my friend, for God is our finisher. You are covered in prayers to fight through and make this study of God's word your priority. All it takes is twenty minutes out of the day, so strategize and commit to the Lord for the next four weeks, and it then will become your lifestyle. Once you have had a taste of living in God's presence daily, you will undoubtedly crave Him more and more.

Day 1: Belt of Truth and Breastplate of Righteousness

Warm-Up: Read Ephesians 6:10–20.

Scripture of Focus:

> Stand your ground, putting on the belt of truth
> and the body armor of God's righteousness.
>
> — Ephesians 6:14

Exercise: How do we stand firm in the belt of truth?

Putting on the belt of truth is preparing us to be Christian warriors in so many ways. The truth we abide by can only come from God's word equipped for us through reading scripture. You see, so many believers feel that listening to sermons once a week is enough. Yes, church is a great way to fellowship, but what happens when we leave the church? People begin to fall back into their everyday routines that exclude studying the scripture for themselves. As we make the decision to transform into God's warriors, we have to become familiar with reciting the Bible verses and meditating on them daily. Memorizing Bible verses can be a great way to tuck God's truth into our belts. The belt of truth will set us free; as John

8:32 states, "And you will know the truth, and the truth will set you free." We all are slaves to sin until we take up the word of God and tuck it into our belts. Studying scripture daily should be a lifestyle and commitment to our Heavenly Father. Reading the Bible is preparation for war that awaits us. As an athlete prepares for games and championships, we must prepare for spiritual battles that lie ahead as well. We must keep our belts of truth on at all times because without them girding us, we will not be equipped to conquer our enemy. Prioritizing God as number one in our hearts is the first step.

> So you must live as God's obedient children. Don't
> slip back into your old ways of living to satisfy your
> own desires. You didn't know any better then.

— 1 PETER 1:14

Now that you know better, it's a must to be better. Just because you go to church and acknowledge our gracious, forgiving Father doesn't mean you can continue living in sinful manners. Exodus 20:7 explains, "You must not misuse the name of the Lord your God. The Lord will not let you go unpunished if you misuse his name." Reading this in context accessed a revelation to my heart about hypocrisy. We must not claim the grace freely given to us by God and then continue acting in a way that brings disgrace to God's character. Living out our actions should be following His decrees in love. We must pay attention to not fall back in the trap of our enemy, falling into old behavior patterns after we repent. When we keep the truth of God tucked into our belts, we can stand taller, walk in obedience, and be set free from the burden of our sins.

How do we put on the breastplate of righteousness?

The breastplate was used as armor to protect a Roman soldier's heart in the physical sense. Contrary to what some people believe, we do not wage war in the physical sense. We walk in the flesh, but war is not according to the flesh. We battle our situations through the spiritual realms as spiritual warriors for God. Like we discussed, Satan is always shooting his flaming arrows at us, so not only does God give us shields, but we are also wearing His breastplates of righteousness. The heart is our most vital organ in all aspects. Physically and spiritually, we will not stay alive without our hearts. Satan knows this, so he aims straight for it.

Let's look at Proverbs 4:23: "Guard your heart above all else, for it determines the course of your life." If our hearts direct the course of our steps, then we must keep God in His rightful seated place reigning over our hearts. This means that if our hearts are corrupted by Satan's arrows, then what flows out of us is like a disease leading to death. When we walk tall with our belt of truth on, we position ourselves to wear the breastplate of righteousness correctly, protecting our hearts. Putting the breastplate on requires us to stay in God's presence daily, not just when we feel like it. We wear the breastplates by walking in obedience to the Lord. Keep in mind, though, you are human and not perfect. God doesn't expect us to be perfect; He just wants our hearts to worship Him.

> For everyone has sinned; we fall short of God's
> glorious standard. Yet God, with undeserved
> kindness, declares that we are righteous.
>
> — ROMANS 3:23–24

God desires to sit on the throne of our hearts so He can do the transforming. Praise the Lord for His kindness and giving you such a gift to access His breastplate of righteousness. He didn't give it to us because we deserved it, but because He loves us so much, He freely gives to us when we ask.

CHALLENGE:

I want you to write down a strategy to stay in the word of God and pray every day. There are so many apps you can download for daily reminders to hear God's word. The word of God is our daily bread; Matthew 6:11 states, "Give us our daily bread." Memorize today's verse and what it does for you. Write it all down in prayer. Use the questions below to help strategize your prayers.

1. How has Satan been preventing you from using your breastplate?

_____

_____

_____

_____

_____

_____

2. How can you move forward from today in God's protection?

_____

_____

_____

_____

_____

_____

_____

Day 2: Shoes of Readiness
Warm-Up: Read Ephesians 6:10–20.

Scripture of Focus:

> For shoes, put on the peace that comes from the
> Good News so that you will be fully prepared.

— Ephesians 6:15

Exercise: Put on the shoes of readiness.
Proper footwear is so important for our day-to-day tasks; whether footwear is for a sport or a job, we have to know the right pair of shoes to put on that day. In the spiritual sense, we have one pair made especially for us: the shoes of peace.

Why is peace so important to wear on our feet? Peace grounds us firmly with Christ as the foundation. The shoes of peace are a gift received as we acknowledge Jesus Christ as our Lord and savior; it allows peace to protect our mind and heart. As Philippians 4:7 states, "Then you will experience God's peace which exceeds anything we can understand. His peace will guard your hearts and minds as you live in Christ Jesus." You see when we have the shoes of peace correctly placed to our feet stepping into battle we stand grounded on a rock solid foundation; we then are ready to serve our God as his warrior. The moment you decide that you truly receive Jesus into your heart, peace is immediately received through the gospel.

> Therefore, since we have been made right in God's
> sight by faith, we have peace with God because
> of what Jesus Christ our Lord has done for us.

> — ROMANS 5:1

It clearly says "by faith," which is why we will discuss faith the whole second week of this study. It is by faith that we allow God to work on our behalf. The shoes of peace are our firm foundation. The gospel we receive into our hearts becomes our firm ground for facing the spiritual battles ahead, which is why protecting our hearts is vital (as we discussed yesterday). God is our rock, so the gospel of peace delivers that rock-solid footing. God is the word, and the word is God.

In the beginning the Word already existed. The
Word was with God, and the Word was God.

—JOHN 1:1

CHALLENGE:

Pray for God's firm foundation to take hold in your heart!
Take God's word of truth, and imprint it on your heart so
that you will have a strong foundation to stand on with the
peace of readiness that comes from the gospel.

1. How can you place your shoes of readiness on?

Being in the word + Prayer

2. Write out all pieces of armor we have discussed thus far,
and wear it well.

Belt of Truth
Breastplate of Righteousness
Shoes of Peace Readiness

DAY 3: SHIELD OF FAITH
Warm-Up: Read Ephesians 6:10–20.

SCRIPTURE OF FOCUS:

> In addition to all of these, hold up the shield
> of faith to stop the fiery arrows of the devil.

> — EPHESIANS 6:16

EXERCISE: PUT ON THE SHIELD OF FAITH.

The shield of faith will protect you from all of the flaming arrows headed toward you. Our enemy Satan is always scheming against us and shooting chaos our way. Our amazing Heavenly Father has equipped us with His shield to use. Yes, you heard right: the shield of faith is our protection. Shield yourself with faith in our Lord. Using God's shield will extinguish the flaming arrows that are meant for our harm. One more important concept to take note of is found in James 2:17: "So you see, faith by itself isn't enough. Unless it produces good deeds, it is dead and useless." What good is our faith if we are not producing good fruit with it? We must continue to obey God, keeping our faith, and worshipping Him.

> Stay alert! Watch out for your great enemy,
> the devil. He prowls around like a roaring
> lion, looking for someone to devour.

> — 1 PETER 5:8

Our enemy is prowling around waiting for an opportunity to arise when we are weak and vulnerable. Remind yourself that in 2 Corinthians 12:9, it says, "My grace is all you need. My power works best in weakness." God's saving grace is sufficient, and the lies of our enemy will never beat us. In the weeks to come, we will discuss all the brave warriors for our Lord who exemplified faith. Faith kept them protected—not perfect—but protected, no matter what was thrown their way. We must walk by faith, not by sight. You will see this throughout the rest of the weeks to come during this study.

CHALLENGE:
Write down how you will put your shield of faith up that cannot be penetrated. Not only does it stop our enemy's arrows, but it also extinguishes the fire. No more lies will hurt us. Your past does not define your future with God. You are forgiven and loved so much. Move forward knowing and proclaiming that you're protected in every way by our mighty God. Write a prayer out using the verse from today. Answer the questions below to help you strategize the prayer.

1. What kinds of arrows do you sense the enemy shooting toward you?

_____ *Sadness* _____

_____ *doubt* _____

_____

_____

_____

_____

2. How can you move forward with your shield up?

Prayer
Word of God
Listening.
Denouncing Satan's plans

For me, I'm shouting from the rooftops that my faith in God will shield all evil from me. I will shout to every problem that I serve a mighty God and will continue to praise Him in any and every storm I'm faced with. Your turn.

DAY 4: HELMET OF SALVATION AND SWORD OF SPIRIT

Warm-Up: Read Ephesians 6:10–20.

SCRIPTURE OF FOCUS:

> Put on salvation as your helmet, and take the
> sword of the spirit, which is the word of God.
>
> — EPHESIANS 6:17

EXERCISE:

Let's visualize that for a second. You are putting the helmet over your head for protection in the physical sense. In the spiritual sense, it will protect your mind. Without our helmets on, the purpose of battle is empty. Knowing whom you serve and the purpose of your battle gives you hope. The helmet of salvation is our heart and mind receiving Jesus as our Lord and Savior. Salvation is not earned but given freely to those who receive it; it is the "free gift of God" (Rom. 6:23). The helmet will protect us from deadly blows to the head spiritually involving discouragement or deceit. Wearing your helmet of salvation allows you to move forward knowing you are loved, worthy, and made for a purpose. You move forward feeling hopeful about your future with the one who created you. All you have to do in order to place the helmet of salvation on is to repent of all your sins and ask Jesus into your heart. Salvation is the ultimate goal for a Christian, and without it we cannot use God's armor and become the warriors He intends for us to be. The sword of the spirit is the word of God. When we are under attack in any battle, the word of God is the most powerful weapon there is.

> For the word of God is alive and powerful.
> It is sharper than the sharpest two-edged
> sword, cutting between soul and spirit,
> between joint and marrow. It exposes
> our innermost thoughts and desires.
>
> — HEBREWS 4:12

The word of God is alive and active, meaning it should be used against our enemy. When we proclaim God's word and promises at our enemy, the victory is ours! Keep reminding yourself the battle we truly face in this life is spiritual. An example of this was given by Jesus in Matthew 16:21–23. Take a second to look up this passage. Jesus explains to His disciples that He will suffer terrible things and be killed. You then hear Peter express how this could not be true. Matthew 16:23 states that Jesus turned to Peter and said, "Get away from me, Satan! You are a dangerous trap to me. You are seeing things merely from a human point of view, not from God's." Jesus was speaking toward Peter, but the message was for Satan because He knew that Peter's human nature had been captivated by Satan's thinking.

> For we are not fighting against flesh-and-blood enemies, but against evil rulers and authorities of the unseen world, against mighty powers in this dark world, and against evil spirits in the heavenly places.

> — EPHESIANS 6:12

CHALLENGE:
If you have never asked Jesus into your heart before or you just need a fresh new start, then I want you to repeat this prayer with me to God. Say it out loud, and write down if you want.

Dear Lord,

I am so grateful for your saving grace. Please forgive me of all my sins. I repent, knowing that you freely will give me the gift of salvation. Please forgive me, Lord. I acknowledge that Jesus died on the cross to take away the burdens of all my wrongdoing. I stand here today in faith ready to say that Jesus Christ is my Lord and Savior. I am ready to be your warrior and fight for you. Thank you for being such a graceful, loving Father and forgiving me.

In Jesus's name I pray,

Amen

> This is good and pleases God our
> Savior, who wants everyone to be saved
> and to understand the truth.
>
> — 1 TIMOTHY 2:3–4

Write out your prayer.

_____

_____

_____

_____

_____

_____

_____

Congratulations on making the greatest decision in this life! Now, we have one more important piece of our armor to discuss. See you tomorrow.

Day 5: Armor Activation
Warm-Up: Read Ephesians 6:10–20.

Scripture of Focus:

> Pray in the spirit at all times and on every
> occasion. Stay alert and be persistent in
> your prayers for all believers everywhere.

> — Ephesians 6:18

Exercise: How do we activate our armor?
Now that you have placed on all six pieces of armor directly given from our Heavenly Father, there is one more principle to discuss. We must activate the armor. The key to activate it and become ready, mighty warriors for our Lord is prayer. Without prayer, the pieces of armor are just bits of metal pieced together. When we pray, the armor becomes activated and unstoppable. Prayer *needs* to be a part of our Christian lifestyle because it is communion with God. It grows our personal relationships with Him. God wants to be in an intimate relationship with you and love on you, but He needs us to choose Him first. God has given you free will to decide who you worship.

Devote yourselves to prayer with an
alert mind and thankful heart.

— Colossians 4:2

Both verses say "to be alert" because we have an enemy prowl-ing. Not only do we pray for ourselves, but it also says to pray for other believers too. We win battles for ourselves and oth-ers by kneeling. Keeling or actions for our Lord is expressing our love to Him with worship. Prayer gives us a sixth sense and allows us to be more watchful. We can see with our spiri-tual eyes and witness things no one else can. Prayer helps us to see what God is needing us to notice. In Colossians, it also says to keep a thankful heart. Thankfulness is the key that unlocks peace. When we continue to grow, being thankful in every situation, we will then continue to have peace in our hearts, which leaves no room for bitterness.

SUMMARY:
Let's discuss how we can move forward from day to day stay-ing armored up for battle. For one thing, we must put God on the throne of our hearts by repenting and receiving the gift of Jesus as our Lord and Savior. After knowing our Savior, we need to learn more about the God we serve by staying in His word daily. Along with reading scripture, we must stay in communion through prayer and worship. Prayer opens the door for talking with God, and worship is the only gift we can give back, showing our grateful hearts. Our actions

displayed should be worship mirroring Jesus. Treating others with kindness and good deeds represents whom you serve. As we move forward, I pray that each day of study, you allow His word to sink deep into your heart, ruling over your own way of living. Allow the word of God to water the seed inside so it will produce much fruit. Leave God in His seated position as number one in your heart.

CHALLENGE:

I challenge you to find time every day for the next three weeks. Plan a time daily when you can read through this study and get to know God more. Now that we have the right armor on and it has been activated, ready for use, we can move forward with our training as warriors. Let's go!

Write out any prayers.

_____

_____

_____

_____

_____

_____

_____

Faith

DAY 1: FAITH LIKE DANIEL

WARM-UP: READ DANIEL 6:1–27.

SCRIPTURE OF FOCUS:

> But when Daniel learned that the law had been
> signed, he went home and knelt down as usual in
> his upstairs room, with its windows open toward
> Jerusalem. He prayed three times a day, just as he
> had always done giving thanks to his God. Then
> the officials went together to Daniel's house and
> found him praying and asking for God's help.
>
> — DANIEL 6:10–11

EXERCISE:

Daniel was faced with one of the biggest problems possible.
He wasn't allowed to pray to God for thirty days. Not only did

he go home and do just that, but he also worshipped, giving thanks to God in the midst of opposition. God tells us in 1 Thessalonians 5:18, "Be thankful in all circumstances, for this is God's will for you who belong to Christ Jesus." Daniel knew that his safest bet would be speaking to the King of all kings and asked God to come into his situation and deliver him. In doing this, he showed a great deal of faith. Can you imagine having that kind of pressure on you? Daniel was already a righteous man who kept his breastplate of righteousness over his heart, so when he was faced with this pressure, his true character was exposed. He showed that he would keep his shield of faith up and allow God to stay seated at the throne of his heart. He continued to worship God despite the consequences. His character was excellent, which is why others became disgruntled and jealous.

Through his *bold* faith, Daniel gave an example of how mighty God truly is and showed how no man should worship anyone other than God. Look at Daniel 6:25: "Then King Darius sent this message to the people of every race and nation and language throughout the world: 'Peace and Prosperity to you! I decree that everyone throughout my kingdom should tremble with fear before the God of Daniel. For he is the living God, and he will endure forever. His kingdom will never be destroyed, and his rule will never end. **He rescues and saves his people; he performs miraculous signs and wonders in the heavens and earth.** He rescued Daniel from the power of the lions.'" We learn that it is by faith and worship that God will protect and care for His people. We not only have *faith* in what

God can do but in who He is: the mighty King of the universe, the Creator of heaven and earth. Just fathom that for a second: the One who breathed life into you and me and the animals around us is the same God who *has control* over your situation, but the question is do you have faith in *Him?* One might ask, "Why would God not put a stop to them throwing him into the den?" God wanted to use Daniel's situation and problem to show how mighty He is. Daniel's struggle grew others' faith because they witnessed the miracle as well. God saw the opportunity to use Daniel to strengthen other people's faith around them. The so-called setback was just the opposite: a setup for the acceleration of God's promises and blessings.

How do we relate to Daniel in our modern-day world now? We feel pressure to serve people and possessions from society! Society teaches our kids to reach for achievements for selfish reasons. Instead of asking our children or other people what they would like to be, we should be asking them who God has created them to become. Our enemy uses society to shift the perspectives in to human views. We as God's warriors have to walk with our spiritual views. Be bold like Daniel, and act in faith.

CHALLENGE:

My challenge for you is to write down your problem on a scrap piece of paper and then pray over it, speaking the word of truth into it and proclaiming that God will deliver you from the mouth of your lion. God is always good and worthy of our praise. God is miraculous and cares for you because He saves

His people. Recite it over and over to yourself and to God. Have faith like Daniel. Keep your prayer about this particular problem somewhere safely written down so you can go back and praise God for answering it. Use the questions below.

1. What lion is standing in your way today, and how can you apply what Daniel exemplified?

_____

_____

_____

_____

_____

_____

_____

2. Tell your lion that your God is mightier than any lion's den you might face. Our God will conquer any issue we encounter or issue that is up ahead. It's all in God's hands. Your God will shut the lion's mouth because He is King of all kings and the Creator of heaven and earth. Speak the word of truth into your problem today. Write it out if necessary.

_____

_____

_____

_____

_____

_____

_____

DAY 2: FAITH IN THE WILDERNESS
Warm-Up: Read Exodus 13:17–22.

SCRIPTURE OF FOCUS:

> When Pharaoh finally let the people go, God
> did not lead them along the main road that runs
> through Philistine territory, even though that
> was the shortest route to the Promise Land. God
> said, "If the people are faced with a battle, they
> might change their minds and return to Egypt."
> So God led them in a roundabout way through
> the wilderness toward the Red Sea. Thus the
> Israelites left Egypt like an army ready for battle.
>
> — EXODUS 13:17–18

EXERCISE:

Firstly, we know that God was taking the Israelites on a detour. The common path from Egypt to Canaan was a straight shot. He specifically says He led them in a roundabout way on purpose. If you look up the definition of detour, it means "going in a roundabout way to avoid something." God was leading them around the shorter route so they would not be faced with the battle that would have been waiting on them down that path. They didn't see what was ahead on that specific path, but God did. He mentioned in scripture that they wouldn't be ready. God knew that the shorter route from Egypt to Canaan is where Egypt's military outposts were. Sometimes God warns us and tries to direct us like he did the Israelites, but we miss the warning and end up defeated.

We learn that God takes care of us and leads us to safe grounds. He will never give us more than we can handle. The sole purpose of the wilderness is explained in Exodus 3:18: "The elders of Israel will accept your message. Then you and the elders must go to the King of Egypt and tell him, 'The Lord, the God of Hebrews, has met with us. So please let us take a three-day journey into the wilderness to offer sacrifices to the Lord, our God.'" This explains God wanted the three-day detour in the wilderness to take place so the people of Israel could learn to worship God. So not only was God keeping the Israelites safe, but He was also teaching them how to worship and grow dependent on Him. Our time frames are different than God's, and sometimes we grow weary because as humans, we instinctively want everything done right away. We live in an instant-gratification type of world. How do we grow if things are given to us right away? The detour is planned by God so that you will be prepared for the battle that is ahead when it is time. I don't necessarily think that the Israelites couldn't have physically battled them, but I think it was more in the mental sense— spiritually, they were not yet ready for battle. Their spiritual muscles wouldn't have been strong enough yet. God used this detour to prepare them and grow their trust in Him as their God. Do you feel stuck in the wilderness or like maybe you have taken a detour on your journey? Please do not grow discouraged. Know that our Creator placed you in that position for your safety, growth, and well-being. It isn't the result of a mistake either. It is designed to build you into the warrior God intends for you to be, so keep the faith. Sometimes the wilderness feels lonely, pointless, and repetitive, and it feels like God's not listening. My friend, the wilderness is for you to grow more dependent on God. Learn to worship God through this hard time, which will open doors for your future. Please know that God will deliver you to your promise land.

TESTIMONIAL PASSAGE:

In my senior year of high school, I was given college scholarship offers to about four Division 1 colleges. I ended up making the best decision I could have in the moment, and I'm going to be honest—it felt so right. My freshman and sophomore years were such a struggle for me mentally as I tried to find my identity as a person and as an athlete. Something always felt off while I was there for two years, and I tried my best to hide my feelings. I fell into depression and worrying about my self-image, thinking that if I just looked better, I would feel better. All these feelings swirled out of control until one night in my apartment my sophomore year, I fell to my knees, inviting God into my mess that I thought I had created. You see, that route I chose was not a mistake; it was the detour God needed me on so I would learn to worship Him. I felt stuck in my decision.

You guys, those stuck feelings didn't come from God but from our enemy; he tries to make us feel ashamed or guilty. Satan tries his hardest to get at you so that you feel worthless. God is so loving and is such a good Father. He so graciously led me back to the promised land because I invited Him in. I began to pray daily, typing out my prayers on my laptop. I then ended up back home, finishing my two collegiate athletic years at the University of Tennessee at Chattanooga. I felt whole again, ending my softball career with great memories and meeting the man who is now my husband. We married and now have two beautiful kids together, which was my promise from God. He delivered me from a sad and lonely place of being in the wilderness. I didn't see it in the moment, but those two years helped me grow into the person I am today. I stopped chasing the wrong things and began chasing God. Worshipping God and seeking Him first led me to my promise. As said in Matthew 6:33, "Seek the kingdom of God above all else, and live righteously, and he will give you everything you need." I'm forever thankful.

CHALLENGE:
Declare how great God is, and know He will deliver you safely out of the wilderness. Even if it seems like it's the wrong plan, know God is still in control and waiting for your heart to open toward Him, asking for His guidance. Pray with an open heart, and let God lead you to your promised land. Use the questions below.

1. What detour do you feel God has placed you in?

    Teaching Middle School

2. What can you learn from the detour for your future?

Day 3: Staying in God's Presence

Warm-Up: Read Exodus 13:17–22.

SCRIPTURE OF FOCUS:

> The Israelites left Succoth and camped at
> Etham on the edge of the wilderness. The Lord
> went ahead of them. He guided them during
> the day with a pillar of cloud, and provided

light at night with a pillar of fire. This allowed
them to travel by day and night. And the Lord
did not move the pillar of cloud or pillar of
fire from its place in front of the people.

— Exodus 13:20–22

EXERCISE:

I want you to visualize what is going on before we discuss it. You
have God's people, the Israelites, walking through the wilderness. The verse says, "He guided them with a pillar of cloud,
and provided light at night with a pillar of fire." A pillar looks
like a cylindrical column from the ground up, so picture that
with clouds during the day and with fire at night. As scripture
describes, this pillar would move from place to place for the
Israelites to know which way was the next path. In modern-day
terms, it was their GPS. When it would move in a certain direction, the Israelites would pack up and move with it.

This shows us that even when God places us in a detour
through the wilderness, He has a plan to lead us through it
until we reach His planned destination. Notice that I said,
"His destination." We sometimes jump ahead of God and
make plans for ourselves. We can avoid that by asking God to
show us His way. The only way the Israelites would have been
able to follow the pillars is by staying in God's presence. This
is where the Israelites had to truly trust God and *His* plan.
Your path will always be aligned with the word of God if the
direction comes from Him.

Your word is a lamp to guide my
feet and a light for my path.

— Psalm 119:105

There will be times when you feel drawn to move in a certain direction. When this happens, pray to God for direction and guidance; James 1:5 states, "If you need wisdom, as our generous God, and He will give it to you. He will not rebuke you for asking." God is the only One who can speak to you about your destination for your particular circumstance. He holds the answer, and when we move without being in the presence of God, we run into big issues. For example, if the Israelites had not listened to God about taking a detour, they wouldn't have been ready to take on the military that was set up ahead on the shorter path. It therefore would have resulted in a big problem. God's will and His presence are never disconnected. I also want to include that we often get complacent in life. We get really comfortable in our situations. When God is telling us to move and follow the pillar, but we stay frozen or locked into our current positions, we get robbed of our dreams because we stay when God told us to move. Dreams are accomplished when we move at the pace of our Lord and in His presence. Even if moving forward seems terrifying, do it anyway. We grow by doing things that feel uncomfortable. When we leap outside our comfort zones, the Lord can work on our behalf because we walk by faith trusting

His way. Our enemy wants to paralyze you with fear, so when you are fearful, cry out to our Lord, and replace your fear with faith.

CHALLENGE:
My challenge for you is to write down your dream or any goals you have. Write a prayer that uses the verses from today's study, and proclaim that God will guide you by day and night with a pillar of cloud and pillar of fire. Have 100 percent trust that His way is the best way, and you're ready to embark on this journey with Him. Let God lead the way!

Write out verse, goals,& Prayer.

_____

_____

_____

_____

_____

_____

_____

_____

_____

_____

_____

_____

_____

_____

DAY 4: FAITH OF A MUSTARD SEED

Warm-Up: Read Matthew 17:14–20.

SCRIPTURE OF FOCUS:

> "You don't have enough faith," Jesus told them.
> "I tell you the truth, if you had faith even as
> small as a mustard seed, you could say to this
> mountain, 'move from here to there,' and it
> would move. Nothing would be impossible."

— MATTHEW 17:20

EXERCISE:

What we hear from this particular passage is that Jesus's disciples were trying to cast out a demon from the boy, and they were unsuccessful in their attempt. They witnessed Jesus do it right after they had tried. It seems as though in the scripture, Jesus gets a little frustrated because they didn't show any faith while they tried to cast out the demon. Jesus then explains to them the capability of moving mountains with only the tiniest bit of faith. He expresses the importance of what faith can do for them and believing that nothing is impossible. I would like to note that the disciples were placing the faith in their human performances instead of Jesus. Imagine what we can do with faith as big as the heavens and earth placed in the *right* source. There is power in the name of Jesus, and I get so fired up thinking about it. You should too. What do we learn about God? Faith is huge in our walk with Him. If we do not have faith, then where do we find any hope? In many instances in the Bible, it is by faith that we are healed, move mountains, and become rescued. Faith is one of the most *vital* components to living a godly, confident life. We just read that God promises us through the mouth of Jesus Himself that when we have faith, *nothing* is impossible—absolutely nothing. Do you see the joy in this?

It all begins with believing in what God is telling you. Believe in His promises, and walk by faith. I'm not saying that there will be an easy road ahead. As a matter of fact, there will probably be more opposition coming your way because our enemy sees how strong our faith is becoming. Nothing makes our enemy boil with anger more than that. What I do know is that God will prepare you for the battles that you are supposed to face, and He will sustain you if you keep your shield of faith in who He is. God Almighty is so powerful and wonderful. His ways are higher than ours, and He has plans that are not meant for our understanding. We must continue to keep the faith.

CHALLENGE:

Take your mountain standing in front of you, and declare your faith in Jesus's powerful name. Then tell your mountain that you will move it because you have faith in our Heavenly Father that is *bigger* than any obstacle you face. Write this down, and speak it out loud. Declare it over and over again, and just watch how God shows up! Use the questions below.

1. Which circumstance comes to mind that almost shattered your faith?

_____

_____

_____

_____

_____

_____

_____

2. Did you place your faith in the wrong source?

_____

_____

_____

_____

_____

_____

_____

3. How can you move forward, placing faith in the right source?

_____

_____

_____

_____

_____

_____

DAY 5: KEEP OUR EYES ON JESUS
Warm-Up: Read Matthew 14:22–33.

SCRIPTURE OF FOCUS:

> "Yes, come," Jesus said. So Peter went over
> the side of the boat and walked on the water
> toward Jesus. But when he saw the strong wind
> and waves, he was terrified and began to sink.
> "Save me, Lord!" he shouted. Jesus immediately
> reached out and grabbed him. "You have so little
> faith," Jesus said. "Why did you doubt me?"
>
> — MATTHEW 14:29–31

EXERCISE:

Let's discuss what just happened during this time. Jesus sent His disciples back home across the waters in their boat while He went up on the mountain to pray by Himself. Jesus spent quite a few hours on the mountain praying, which means the boat was long gone from the land. The disciples started to experience some heavy winds and waves during their travels, and this started to place fear in their minds. Then they suddenly saw Jesus standing on the water walking toward them. They were so terrified that they weren't sure if they were seeing a ghost or Jesus, so Peter decided to be bold and ask Jesus to confirm His presence.

Jesus will always sustain us and hold us up, even when we doubt Him the tiniest bit. We also learn that Jesus sometimes can feel so far away from us during our times of struggle, but in reality, He is right there with us waiting to hear the words, "Help me, Lord," like Peter expressed. Too often, we hear God telling us to step out of the boat, meaning to move out of our comfort zones with faith into the unknown. The first minute we obey, we start second-guessing God's plan or our abilities, or we even undervalue our worth. We start playing in our heads all the things that can go wrong. For a minute we forget to enjoy the process because we don't immediately see the result. Why? We lose our focus on Jesus. Reread the passage describing when Peter stepped out of the boat. Peter first saw the wind and waves, causing him to take his eyes off Jesus, which allowed doubt to creep into his mind. That split second of taking your eyes off Jesus can cause you to get lost and magnify the problems around instead of magnifying God. We have to keep our eyes on Jesus the whole time. How do we do that? We uproot every distraction there is and stay in the word of God. Stay in His presence, worshipping and praising Him. These three things are vital to staying in God's presence: read His word, pray, and worship. Peter started to sink only because of his doubt but was sustained by shouting for help with the powerful name of Jesus. God will never abandon you. Deuteronomy 31:8 states, "Do not be afraid or discouraged, for the Lord will personally go ahead of you. He will be with you; He will neither fail you nor abandon you."

CHALLENGE:

My challenge for you is to declare to our enemy—who has placed distractions in your way—that you no longer acknowledge his schemes. You declare that our God will sustain us and keep us walking on water hand in hand with Jesus, our Savior! Declare that in the powerful name of Jesus, you will do the impossible. You will seek Jesus and keep your eyes fixed on Him alone. Watch how God moves in the next adventure He's calling you toward! Answer the questions below.

1. Are you magnifying your problem or God? Explain.

_____

_____

_____

_____

_____

_____

2. Are you letting fear sink you? How do you prevent sinking?

_____

_____

_____

_____

_____

_____

3. How can you use the shield of faith to keep you sustained?

_____

_____

_____

_____

_____

_____

_____

Confidence

——— ⊶∞∞ ———

DAY 1: CONFIDENCE LIKE DAVID
WARM-UP: READ 1 SAMUEL 17:1–57.

SCRIPTURE OF FOCUS:

> As Goliath moved closer to attack, David
> quickly ran out to meet him. Reaching into
> his Shepherd's bag and taking out a stone, he
> hurled it with his sling and hit the Philistine in
> the forehead. The stone sank in, and Goliath
> stumbled and fell face down on the ground.
>
> — 1 SAMUEL 17:48-49

EXERCISE:

As we read through the passage, we learn that David was a
shepherd boy who would go back and forth from watching
his father's sheep in Bethlehem to accompanying Saul's army

when he could. David had older brothers who were in Saul's army. We see young David hearing of the taunts from this Goliath, the Philistine champion of Gath. David becomes frustrated that Goliath would chant his usual taunt and defy the army of the living God. This simply means Goliath would shout toward God and His people, challenging them to battle. David told Saul that he would stand up to this pagan Philistine because God had prepared him. We then witness David do exactly that—conquer Goliath with only a sling and stone. He opted out of wearing any of Saul's physical armor because he had the living God working through him.

Don't ever let man tell you that you cannot accomplish something that you know is a divine command from our Heavenly Father. Choosing obedience to God trumps having experience any day! Placing our confidence in the Lord is trusting Him in every situation we encounter. When we know that God is asking us to do something challenging, we need to remember 2 Corinthians 12:9: "Each time He said, 'My grace is all you need. My power works best in weakness.' So now I am glad to boast about my weaknesses, so that power of Christ can work through me." God will never ask you to do something that He hasn't prepared you for. God prepared David for this battle during his previous years of watching over sheep. As mentioned, David explained how he was used to slaying lions and bears while protecting the sheep and goats. David didn't place his confidence in himself, though; he placed it in the living God who dwelled in him. You have the same mighty God dwelling inside of you too. You just have to learn to activate the warrior found within. Prayer, the word of God, and worship all help you tap into divine strength and courage. Christ's power rests inside you when you acknowledge Jesus and how powerful He truly is.

At some point in your life, you will encounter struggles. Don't mistake a closed door from God for a jammed door. That resistance you face may feel like a setback in your life, but in reality, it's just strengthening you to dig deeper to receive the divine power of our living God that dwells inside you. You will then grow into a warrior with divine courage and strength. The obstacle or setback will actually propel you forward when the time is right. Trust God in the process, even when you don't see the end result. Allow God to shoot you, His warrior arrow, into the giant when His timing is right. God's timing is always perfect! Know it, and believe it.

CHALLENGE:
Next time you are faced with a giant taunting you, you declare to it out loud that your mighty God is living inside you and will knock it down with one shot. You tell Goliath with boldness that his lies of telling you that you aren't worthy enough, pretty enough, or enough of anything is not going to stop you. You call his bluff, and you will defeat him because the divine, living God who loves you, adores you, and protects you lives inside you. You are unstoppable! Declare this out loud in prayer, and write it down to remind yourself how you have God working through you just like David did. Speak truth into your giant today!

1. How can you step up to your next challenge?

_____

_____

_____

_____

_____

_____

_____

2. How can you show your confidence in who God says He is like David did?

_____

_____

_____

_____

_____

_____

_____

DAY 2: UNDER PRESSURE

Warm-Up: Read Isaiah 41:8–13.

SCRIPTURE OF FOCUS:

> Don't be afraid, for I am with you. Don't
> be discouraged, for I am your God. I will

strengthen you and help you. I will hold
you up with My victorious right hand.

— ISAIAH 41:10

EXERCISE:

God is encouraging the Israelites with a command and promise. He is reminding them they are His servants and are governed by Him. If you reread verses 8 and 9, God is reminding them He chose them because He wanted to. He didn't choose them because of their achievements or anything they had done on their own. Just like he chose Jacob, an untrustworthy con man, God is expressing to the Israelites that they should not fear because He is with them. He plans to strengthen them and uphold them with His righteous right hand. You are not supposed to be perfect. It is okay to not have it all together, and being a big mess is acceptable.

God wants us to be encouraged by what He can do for us and through us. God promises us He will uphold and strengthen us. When we feel burdened by pressure, we need to remember that we are chosen despite our imperfectness. Repeat Psalm 139:13–14 to yourself: "You made all the delicate, inner parts of my body and knit me together in my mother's womb." God will never send you through something He didn't prepare you for because He loves you and will protect you. When you face trials of various kinds, you must stay focused on the One who created you for that obstacle.

He knows you better than you know yourself. We learn that our confidence must be placed in God and not ourselves—like Peter taking his eyes off Jesus for a split second, causing him to sink. Do not take your eyes off Jesus. Our human performance can only go so far without the living God working in us. John 15:4–5 states, "Remain in me, and I will remain in you. For a branch can not produce fruit if it is severed from the vine, and you cannot be fruitful unless you remain in me."

In today's world there is pressure rising around us in every direction. Pressure takes place when we carry around burdens that can suffocate us. As humans, when we face pressured situations, we instinctively react too fast from panic and end up making mistakes. When we are burdened by pressure, our true characteristics will be exposed. If we stay in the word of God with prayer, surrendering all our burdens, then we expose Jesus to the problem, and it ceases. Pressure makes us fear the outcome, and God reminds us abundantly not to fear. It is a command, not a suggestion.

CHALLENGE:
I challenge you to surrender to Gods any cares that place pressure on you. He can take it; He promises us that. Declare that God is upholding you and will fight for you.

> In my distress I prayed to the Lord, Lord
> answered me and set me free. The Lord
> is for me, so I will have no fear.
>
> — PSALM 118:5–6

Declare this verse to your pressure point, and hold tight to God's promises. He is a faithful promise keeper and will set you free.

1. What do you need to be set free from?

_____

_____

_____

_____

_____

_____

_____

2. How can you allow God to set you free from pressure?

_____

_____

_____

_____

_____

_____

_____

Day 3: Self-Confidence
Warm-Up: Read Exodus 3:7–4:17.

Scripture of Focus:

> Then the Lord asked Moses, "Who makes
> a person's mouth? Who decides whether

people speak or do not speak, hear or do
not hear, see or do not see? Is it not I, the
Lord? Now go! I will be with you as you speak,
and I will instruct you I what to say."

— EXODUS 4:11-12

EXERCISE:

Moses was approached by God through a burning bush one
day. He was there to tell Moses the plans for delivering His
people from slavery into the promised land. As we have covered in week 2, God wanted to send the people of Israel into
the wilderness for three days so they could learn how to sacri-
fice for the Lord. Moses rebuked this a few times, explaining
that he didn't feel equipped to do what God was calling him
to do. Moses tried to make excuses to justify why he shouldn't
be the one to perform this assignment. How many times do
we act in the same manner toward God? God then reminds
Moses that He will be with him, and there isn't any need to
be afraid. Moses still wants to argue with God about how he
gets his words twisted and cannot speak. God then appoints
Aaron, Moses's older brother, to be his voice when they go to
Pharaoh. Moses and Aaron did as God said.

The Lord created us, and we should not question His
authority when we are given tasks from Him. Moses clearly
had self-esteem issues with the way he spoke. He was inse-
cure about his word choice and structure. Those insecurities held Moses back from speaking for God. When we pass

something up, God will find someone to get the job done. Do not let your insecurities hold you back from being a part of something great for God's glory. God is our self-esteem booster. When we feel like God has asked us to do something, we need to place our hope in who *He* is. We are made in the image of God: "So God created human beings in his own image. In the image of God he created them; male and female he created them" (Gen. 1:27). Exodus 15:3 states, "The Lord is a warrior; Yahweh is his name!" If we are made to be like God, then we, too, are warriors at heart. In order to activate the warriors inside of us, we must invite God in and stay in His presence daily. The God who resurrected Jesus from death is the same God living inside you.

> The spirit of God, who raised Jesus from the dead,
> lives in you. And just as God raised Christ Jesus
> from the dead, He will give life to your mortal
> bodies by this same spirit living within you.
>
> — ROMANS 8:11

Therefore, if we decide to show God how grateful we are for having access to such godly confidence, then we need to act it out. Actions speak louder than words. They always have and always will because they produce worship for our Heavenly Father.

Choose to listen for the Lord, and move when He says to move. If God needs you to speak up, then do as He says.

The only time you will fall is when you put hope and confidence in your own human performance. When we place our hope in who God is and what He is capable of doing through us, we will conquer anything standing in our way because the living God is working inside of us, activating our inner warriors. The key for self-confidence is having confidence in God and in the fact that you are made in His image. You are His warrior, fulfilling His purpose here on earth.

CHALLENGE:
Write out your own prayer for declaring God's promises to you. If you have been asked to do a task and feel unworthy or unequipped, then remind yourself of God's promises; speak the word of God to your doubt, using a Bible verse from today's study. You are God's warrior. Allow Him to work through you to fight the good fight and finish what He started.

1. How can you be a self-confident warrior?

_____

_____

_____

_____

_____

_____

_____

DAY 4: FRUIT OF THE HOLY SPIRIT
Warm-Up: Read Galatians 5:16–5:23.

Scripture of Focus:

> But the Holy Spirit produces this kind of fruit
> in our lives: love, joy, peace, patience, kindness,
> goodness, faithfulness, gentleness, and self-
> control. There is no law against these things!
>
> — Galatians 5:22-23

Exercise:

In this passage you read that we are to live according to the Holy Spirit and not our own fleshly desires. When we accept Jesus into our hearts, we then allow the Lord to reside in us through the Holy Spirit. The verse above says the Holy Spirit produces all kinds of good fruit. It doesn't say our human nature produces fruit. Humanly speaking, our ways are corrupt and sinful. We must tap into the spiritual realms by prayer, which allows our inner spiritual warriors to be activated. Our sinful ways desire things of this world that do not align with God's word. We must seek God's will. Psalm 37:4 states, "Take delight in the Lord, and he will give you your heart's desires." The minute you receive Jesus into your heart and start to live for His purpose, you will allow the Holy Spirit to be active and dwell in your heart forever. Now take note that there is a difference in allowing God to dwell in your heart and actually activating the Holy Spirit to work through you. For example, you can live a life loving and believing God but not actually living with the Holy Spirit activated. If the Holy Spirit is not activated, then you will continue to live according to your own fleshly desires. When we stay armored up like we discussed in week 1, we stay on guard waiting for the Lord to guide us. The word of God keeps us in line. Satan is creative in his work because he can manipulate you into picking an "almost-right" decision versus a right one. Confirming your answer by the Bible is how you know which is the divine right. As it states in 2 Timothy 3:16, "All scripture is inspired by God and useful to teach us what is true and to make us realize what is wrong in our lives. It corrects us when we are wrong and teaches us to do what is right."

TESTIMONIAL PASSAGE:
I want to share with you how Satan is sneaky in disguising himself. Satan tries to turn your blessing into a burden through many methods. He will try to replace God on the throne in your heart. What do I mean? I'm referring to when we get so busy going through our everyday lives that we sometimes can replace God's position with worry, doubt, fear, hobbies, sports, jobs, and so forth. Those things become our idols. For example, if we replace God on the throne with our jobs, then we will end up hating our work lives, and this flows out toward other people. When we keep the fresh breath of God speaking into our hearts, we stay refreshed. We find more joy. It angers me to know that Satan tries to guilt us into saying yes to everything. God doesn't call us to say yes all the time. We need to realize it's okay to say no to certain things that aren't priorities in that season of life. I will never forget when my friend asked me to keep her newborn baby while I myself had a six-month-old daughter. I was still new to being a mommy

in general, but I felt guilty if I didn't say yes to her. It was a disaster; keeping two babies that close in age was exhausting, and I couldn't enjoy anything that day. Fortunately, my friend was sweet and understanding, and she didn't hold it against me when I explained I couldn't manage this request. I learned from that moment that sometimes saying no is good for our health both mentally and physically. It brings more joy to our seasons of life. Satan wants you to feel guilty and stay busy so you will miss the other arrows coming your way. If he has you occupied being busy, then you will forget to put your breastplate on—which is vital for protection over your heart!

CHALLENGE:

I challenge you to set a plan in action in which you write down a prayer daily to God, asking Him to change your heart's desires. Pray for God to make your desires align with His purpose and will for your life. Repent to God for selfishly seeking your own ways, and admit your fault. Then thank God for His amazing grace, and move forward knowing that God will lead you by the Holy Spirit if you choose to follow Him.

1. How can we choose God daily?

_____

_____

_____

_____

_____

_____

_____

2. How do we allow the fruit of the spirit to work through us?

_____

_____

_____

_____

_____

_____

_____

DAY 5: CONFIDENCE THIEF
Warm-Up: Read John 10:6–10.

SCRIPTURE OF FOCUS:

> The thief's purpose is to steal and
> kill and destroy. My purpose is to give
> them a rich and satisfying life.

— JOHN 10:10

PASSAGE SUMMARY:

Jesus was explaining a parable, an explanation of a story, about the shepherd and his sheep. Read through the passage a few times yourself, and then come back. He is saying He watches over His sheep, referring to those who follow Him. He will always care for His sheep. The sheep trust His leadership and follow Him. Jesus is the gatekeeper and keeps away those who might harm His sheep; He keeps His flock inside the pen where they can safely remain under His protection. We stay protected by our gatekeeper, Jesus. Jesus warns us that there is an enemy who has a game plan to hinder us and destroy us. As long as we draw near to Jesus and follow Him, we will never perish.

EXERCISE:

God knows our enemy will be out to get us in every way. Thankfully, God decided to gift us the only present worth receiving: "For God loved the world so much that he gave his one and only Son, so that everyone who believes in him will not perish but have eternal life" (John 3:16). God loves us that much. Think about that for a second. You are so loved. Can you guess who attempts to steal your confidence? Our one true enemy, Satan. He is the only thief around who purposely brings grief and chaos into your life. Satan is so clever that he will disguise himself, appearing to us through different methods. The biggest disguise I see him using is the game of comparison. He will get so sneaky as to make you start comparing yourself to others—their lives, their accomplishments, their looks. He uses social media for his platform. How many times have you looked on your social media account to see someone portraying how perfect his or her life is? How does that make you feel about your life? Exactly. Do you know why Satan is in attempt to drag us down? He desires to be worshipped. He sees our praises to God and continues to strategize against our hearts. Satan knows how important you are to our Heavenly Father. Satan slowly starts to take away the joy you have from your own path, which is uniquely made for you. You then lose your own identity and start chasing the wrong things, all because of the distraction of comparison. I want you to read Galatians 6:4: "Pay careful attention to your own work, for then you will get the satisfaction of a job well done, and you won't need to compare yourself to anyone else. For we are each responsible for our own conduct." The only applause we need comes from God. He does not want you comparing your life to someone else's. Your work, talents, and accomplishments do not need the approval of this world. We all have our gifts from the Lord to be treasured. Know that you are great, loved, worthy, and capable of moving mountains when you keep the faith. Keep Jesus as your focus, and allow Him to protect you like He has promised. Keep your eyes fixed on our gatekeeper, Jesus.

CHALLENGE:
My challenge for you is to write down a verse that stuck out to you from today! Use Post-it notes, or write it in an agenda that you keep nearby. Remind yourself that Jesus is the way and that His applause is all you need in this life. You want God to say, "Job well done." We will not let Satan steal any more of our confidence because we will continue to place it in God alone. Proclaim God's goodness, and believe it.

1. What is your confidence thief?

_____

_____

_____

_____

_____

_____

_____

2. How can you protect your confidence?

_____

_____

_____

_____

_____

_____

_____

Perseverance

———— ∞∞ ————

DAY 1: STEWARD WELL
WARM-UP: READ LUKE 5:1–11.

SCRIPTURE OF FOCUS:

> For he was awestruck by the number of fish they
> had caught, as were the others with Him.

— LUKE 5:9

EXERCISE:

Jesus was preaching one day on the shore of the Sea of Galilee. Jesus asked to use Simon's boat to preach the word from the boat to the great crowds pressing on Him. When Jesus initially asked to use the boat, Simon Peter was washing his net because they had been fishing all night and had not caught one single fish. Then, after Jesus was done preaching, He commanded Simon Peter to go out into deeper waters and let down the nets; Simon Peter replied, "Master, we worked hard all last night and didn't catch a thing. But if you say so, I'll let the nets down again" (Luke 5:5). Their nets then filled up with so many fish they had to shout for help because it was in abundance. They were so amazed at what Jesus did that they felt undeserving.

Simon Peter could have very well given up! He could have said no to Jesus and not believed. He chose to listen and continue to work hard, despite the results from the previous night. Simon, whose name later changes to Peter, is a well-known fisherman and knew what he was doing, so he and the other fishermen probably thought Jesus was silly for asking them to let the nets down again. They believed and did it anyway. They knew the circumstances were not ideal for catching fish. Colossians 3:23–24 states, "Work willingly at whatever you do, as though you were working for the Lord rather than for people. Remember that the Lord will give you an inheritance as your reward, and that the Master you are serving is Christ." This is stewarding well with what you've already been given. Persevere and work hard with all of your heart for God's glory. Being faithful, hard workers for the Lord should be our goal. Even during the hard days of work, school, or practice when situations don't seem ideal, you fight through. Continue to steward well through the hard days, being faithful to God. Sometimes God will call us to swim through deep waters, so keep swimming because our obedience will allow God Almighty to move on our behalf. God just wants us to persevere with our hearts and work ethics and keep our faith in who God is. Sometimes the circumstances will not always make sense, but when we believe in Jesus and listen to Him, the road will be worth it. We have to embrace the process with Jesus to experience the promise. When we sit back and make excuses, we second-guess our Heavenly Father.

CHALLENGE:
I challenge you to remind yourself today for whom you are going to work. You are made by Almighty God to do good work, whatever it may be. You have the opportunity to let God's goodness work through you for those you encounter in day-to-day activities. Give God the glory, and let His light shine through you. Steward well over whatever job you have been given or whatever opportunity has been placed in front of you. Utilize what you have been given, and persevere, even if it doesn't seem fair. God is seeing your heart work and will not forsake you.

1. What has God given you to steward well over?

_____
_____
_____
_____
_____
_____
_____

Day 2: From Prison to Promotion
Warm-Up: Read Genesis 39:19–23 and Genesis 41:40.

Scripture of Focus:

> Pharaoh sent for Joseph at once, and he was
> quickly brought from the prison. After he shaved
> and changed his clothes, he went in and stood
> before Pharaoh. Then Pharaoh said to Joseph,
> "I had a dream last night, and no one here can can
> tell me what it means. But I have heard that when
> you hear about a dream you can interpret it."
> "It is beyond my power to do this,"
> Joseph replied. "But God can tell you
> what it means and set you at ease."
>
> — Genesis 41:14-16

Exercise:
Let's do a quick review on what is going on. Joseph was sold into slavery by his brothers because of jealousy. He then was put in prison for being accused of being intimate with his master's wife. Joseph clearly was not at fault through any of these unfair circumstances, but God still had a plan. The Lord never left Joseph, and during his time in jail, the warden placed him in charge of the other prisoners. He was placed in a leadership role, and he succeeded in everything he did

there because the Lord never left him. Fast-forward to now; Pharaoh had heard about this man named Joseph who could interpret dreams. Pharaoh request him to be pulled out of the prison to come and interpret his dream. Joseph does just that and offers wise advice on how to strategize a plan for what was to come. Read verse 40: "You will be in charge of my court, and all my people will take orders from you. Only I, sitting on my throne, will have a rank higher than yours." We see that Pharaoh was so pleased with Joseph's helpful wisdom from God that he then placed him over his entire court.

God never left Joseph throughout the entire journey of his struggles. Joseph was in prison for two years, which seemed like a huge setback. In reality, though, the Lord allowed this setback to strengthen Joseph's character and prepare him for the battle ahead. Joseph always made the best of his circumstances and never complained. He continued to trust the Lord, persevering through the unfair times and knowing that God would fulfill His promises to deliver him.

> For God is pleased with you when
> you do what you know is right and
> patiently endure unfair treatment.

> — 1 Peter 2:19

Sometimes in life we can feel stuck or feel like there is no hope in the midst of our chaos. Think of yourself as an arrow. God is going to pull you back before He releases you, but when He does release, be ready for the acceleration of blessings. God placed Joseph in leadership roles during his time in jail, which allowed him to develop leadership skills for when Pharaoh promoted him later on. He didn't have to apply for it; They called for Him! God is so good.

> You will be in charge of my court, and all my
> people will take orders from you. Only I, sitting
> at my throne, will have a rank higher than you.
>
> — GENESIS 41:40

CHALLENGE:

I want you to think of times when you felt like you were having a setback or there was an obstacle in your way preventing you from succeeding. Write out your prayer proclaiming that God has a big plan ahead to prosper you and not to harm you. Shout to your obstacle that you will persevere through and that God will accelerate you when it is time to be released! Remember this verse: "Jesus replied, 'You don't understand now what I am doing, but someday you will.'" (John 13:7).

1. What obstacle or unfair situation are you facing now?

_____

_____

_____

_____

_____

_____

_____

2. How can you use this in the future?

_____

_____

_____

_____

_____

_____

_____

DAY 3: WHY PERSEVERE?
Warm-Up: Read Romans 5:1–5.

SCRIPTURE OF FOCUS:

> We can rejoice, too, when we run into
> problems and trials, for we know that they
> help us develop endurance. And endurance
> develops strength of character, character
> strengthens our confident hope of salvation.
>
> — ROMANS 5:3–4

EXERCISE:
Right off the bat, we read that we have been made right in God's eyes by faith. Faith in God and His promises provides peace for our hearts. Paul is explaining to us through this passage that God loves us so much, and we need to celebrate with

a secure understanding. There is nothing that can ever separate us from the love of and relationships with our Heavenly Father. We will have trials and struggles that we must deal with in this life: "Yes, and everyone who wants to live a godly life in Christ Jesus will suffer persecution" (2 Tim. 3:12). God never promised us glorious, problem-free lives. He wants us to lose ourselves and take up Jesus, even while knowing we will face hard times, opposition, and suffering during our time here on earth. As difficult as it gets, we must remain faithful to the things we have been taught.

> You have been taught the holy scriptures
> from childhood, and they have given you
> the wisdom to receive the salvation that
> comes by trusting in Christ Jesus.
>
> — 2 Timothy 3:15

Although we know suffering will happen, we must remember that Jesus has overcome the world, so there is no need to fear. We have received a *gift* of eternal life through Jesus, which is our main focus—or should be—in our lifetimes. Each morning we should wake up clothed in gratitude to our Lord and spend the day doing what is pleasing to Him.

EXERCISE:
Kneel in prayer to our Lord, and let Him know you choose Him daily and want to do what is pleasing to His will and

plans (even if it means sitting at a desk for certain number of years, know that God has a purpose for you there). Keep working hard for the Lord, no matter where He has planted you. He's got a purpose for *everything*!

1. What moment can you describe through which you had to persevere?

_____

_____

_____

_____

_____

_____

_____

2. How can you remember this and allow this focus of scripture to help you in the future?

_____

_____

_____

_____

_____

_____

_____

DAY 4: BE BOLD
Warm-Up: Read 2 Timothy 1:1–18.

SCRIPTURE OF FOCUS:

> For God has not given us a spirit of fear and
> timidity, but of power, love, and self-discipline.

— 2 TIMOTHY 1:7

EXERCISE:

Timothy was left in Ephesus to preach the gospel because the people there were involved with false teachings. Timothy was unsure whether he was equipped to do the job and wanted to flee the town. Paul reminded Timothy over and over again that he was doing great and was able to accomplish the job, relying on God to work through him. Keep in mind that Paul was in jail as he continued to pray and encourage Timothy to do God's work and bring glory to His name. Timothy was teaching all of the people in Ephesus the word of God and what it meant to be a faithful follower.

God wants us to be *bold* in our faith like Paul was and share the good news when we have the moments and opportunities to do so! Thankfully, God fills our soul with the Holy Spirit because of Christ. That means when we seek God and His kingdom before all else, He will fill us up with *love, power,* and *self-discipline*! This is why I strongly believe that God has to be a part of our everyday lives. He is our lifestyle to live out on a daily basis. It is through Christ that we have the self-discipline we need to conquer our goals. When we try to do it ourselves, we must remember we are human and will fail because only with God can the *right* self-discipline be acquired. Trust me, I have tried it my own way in the past and have wound up weak, depressed, or just in constant defeat mode because I am a weak-minded human without the Lord's strength. There is so much supernatural power in Jesus's name, so we must *believe* it! Even when it is something as simple as making your daily decisions boldly, ask God to give you the willpower and discipline you need to get it done for His glory—not because you want to gain the approval of others but simply because you want to thank our Heavenly Father for this life He's gifted you with. Steward well over the opportunities that God delivers. Honor Him through your actions, which will show worship. No matter how fearful you become, persevere.

> Patient endurance is what you need now, so
> that you will continue to do God's will. Then
> you will receive all that He has promised.
>
> — HEBREWS 10:36

CHALLENGE:
Boldly pray this verse to God, and show Him your faith in all He promises! Share with God that you will be Strong in His name and will not let fear or timidity *ever* take you over because our God is so much bigger, and He loves us infinitely!

1. How can you put on a spirit of faith?

_____

_____

_____

_____

_____

_____

_____

2. How can you choose faith over fear and be bold in the future?

_____

_____

_____

_____

_____

_____

_____

DAY 5: OUR WHY

Today is our final day of this study, and there are several principles I would like to review as we come to a close. I pray that after ending this study, you move forward with a refreshed view of what it means to hold a relationship with our Lord and Savior! Repent, and accept Jesus into your heart. He doesn't want us to change before coming to receive our gifts. God wants us as we are, imperfect but willing. God just wants us to invite Him into our lives. We are made to be God's warriors, and figuring it out is half the battle. If you realize whose you are, you will be left on the right path that leads to knowing more about God and leaves you understanding who He made you to be. Three components to remember for your time with the Lord to strengthen your spiritual muscles are to read God's word, worship, and pray! We all have spiritual athletic ability in our souls for Christ, waiting to be awakened: "And athletes cannot win the prize unless they follow the rules" (2 Tim. 2:5). Our only prize is eternal life with our Heavenly Father. God's plan is given in Ephesians 2:10: "For we are God's masterpiece, created in Christ Jesus to do good works, which God prepared in advance for us to do." Every single moment in your life has been planned to establish you. You are a masterpiece. The pieces that you thought were unworthy are used by God to build you into a beautiful warrior. We all will have scars, but those scars are beautiful reminders of an amazing God working for your good.

> "For I know the plans I have for you," says the
> Lord, "They are plans for good and not for
> disaster, to give you a future and a hope."
>
> — JEREMIAH 29:11

As your transformation begins, I pray you remember to armor up, keep your faith, place confidence in our Father, and persevere. Those four things will allow you to finish the race and fight the good fight. As Hebrews 12:1–2 states, "Therefore, since we are surrounded by such a huge crowd of witnesses to the life of faith, let us strip off every weight that slows us down, especially the sin that so easily trips us up. And let us run with endurance the race God has set before us. We do this by keeping our eyes on Jesus, the champion who initiates and perfects our faith. Because of the joy awaiting Him, He endured the cross, disregarding its shame. Now He is seated in the place of honor beside God's throne." Now rise up, Warrior!

Dear Heavenly Father,
Please know how privileged and honored we feel to be Your mighty warriors. We will endure the race before us with Your mighty courage and strength. Please bless us with the wisdom and knowledge that only comes from You so we can keep our behaviors and actions aligned with Your will, Lord. We love You with every bit of our beings, and our focus is You daily. We will move forward in this life fighting for Your victory. Thank You for all You have already blessed us with in this life.
In Jesus's name we pray,
Amen

Use the lines below to write out your prayer moving forward as God's Warrior!

_____

_____

_____

_____

_____

ACKNOWLEDGMENTS

I OWE A DEBT OF love to my whole family for all their support. Thank you to Ben, my two kids: Emmett& Kailani, Mom, Dad, my baby sister, her husband Josh, and my Aunt Tina. You all have been so supportive throughout this whole process and I am forever grateful. A huge thank you goes out to close friends that prayed and cheered me on as well. Megan Wright, my baby sister, and her husband Josh Wright did a phenomenal job in their photography skills to help create the perfect book cover. I would also like to express my thankful heart to everyone at Elite Authors. Your work on editing and especially the help of designing the book was amazing work. You all made this process super fun and joyful. Thank you all from the bottom of my heart! God is so good.

28721931R00044

Made in the USA
Lexington, KY
19 January 2019